Earth People's Park

Earth People's Park

A Memoir of the Counter-Culture

Morgan M. Morgan

with

Eric Leif Davin

Davinbooks
P.O. Box 90087
Pittsburgh, PA 15224

Earth People's Park
A Memoir of the Counter-Culture

Originally a chapter in
Orphans of the Storm
A Shared Memoir of the Radical Seventies
2020

Cover: Morgan in the Seventies
Photo by Eric Leif Davin

Dedication

To my beautiful wife, Abbe, who completes me. To our children, Aric, Ian, Vanessa, Caitlin, Cole, and Cassidy, who fulfill my life. To our grandchildren, Leia, Olivia, Amyia, Dalia, and Lamarie. To our great-grandchildren, Le'Aiylah, Aviannah, Ajalei, and Lillyanna, who bring such joy.

Also, to Lobo, my partner for all those years on the streets, and who traveled all those miles with me.

And to my brothers, especially Eric Leif Davin, who kept pushing me to get my memoirs written before I die. His help with writing, editing, typing, and morale boosting made it all possible.

And, lastly, to my brothers and sisters on the streets, especially the STP Family. Brothers and Sisters to the end.

VENCEREMOS!

Earth People's Park

June-September, 1973

Eric: The Hog Farm was a traveling commune founded in the late Sixties based, variously, in Los Angeles, New Mexico, and New York. It was a community-service oriented commune that provided support facilities, such as first aid, food, and crisis intervention, at rock festivals. Perhaps its most well known activity was when it filled this role at the Woodstock festival in the summer of 1969. The public spokesperson for the Hog Farm was an ex-comedian named Hugh Romney who went under the name of Wavy Gravy, and Wavy Gravy took the microphone many times to make announcements at Woodstock.

In the wake of Woodstock, the Hog Farm conceived the idea of Earth People's Park, taking its name from Berkeley's People's Park. The original idea was to buy a tract of about 5,000 acres somewhere in northern New Mexico, perhaps around Taos, which would be made available to anyone who wanted to come and live on it for free in an alternative life style. The money for the purchase would come from a huge rock concert held on the proposed land itself.

That project never came to fruition, so the plan was altered to the creation of many small versions of Earth People's Park all over the country. The Hog Farm toured the nation trying to drum up enough money for this venture. Despite the herculean logistical and financial problems, the Hog Farm was finally able, in 1970, to incorporate and create at least one such Earth People's Park in northern Vermont's Essex County. For $38,000 they bought 592 wooded acres outside the town of Norton, right on the Canadian border. You could take a walk in the woods and accidentally end up in Canada. For many on the street, it was said to be the much-desired anarchic Garden of Eden that so many of them sought.

Earth People's Park survived haphazardly for twenty years. Then, in 1990, a gang of biker-junkies moved into the hippie enclave and took over. They began clear cutting the forest with chain saws in order to sell timber to support their heroin habits and their wallets. Those few hippies who remained were either intimidated into silence, or driven off.

Wavy Gravy was notified, and he contacted Tony Serra, the Earth People's Park attorney who had set everything up originally. Serra sent a legal notice to the bikers, the timber buyers, the police, the U.S. Border Patrol, and anyone else he could think of, that the logging was illegal and should immediately cease. The logging was stopped, but the biker gang continued to occupy Earth People's Park and continued to deal drugs and intimidate anyone who objected. Federal agents infiltrated the park and one of the bikers sold some drugs to a federal undercover agent. The ensuing raid uncovered an arsenal of weapons and over $10,000 in cash. The federal agents evicted the biker gang from the park and made arrests.

Because of drug forfeiture laws, this incident led to the end of Earth People's Park. The federal government seized the park in October, 1990, evicted the remaining tenants, and demolished all structures. The land was eventually transferred to the state of Vermont on October 5th, 1994, and is now known as Black Turn Brook State Forest. It is open to the public for hunting, fishing, hiking, and camping. However, vehicle access is restricted and no permanent structures are allowed. In a way, therefore, the land that was formerly Earth People's Park still belongs to the people.

****

Morgan: Living on the street as part of the Seventies counter-culture was just one damn thing after another, with no particular place to go and nothing in particular to do, except party and get high. We drifted hither and yon, from place to place, whenever and wherever the mood took us.

One of the main places we hung out was Harvard Square, in Cambridge, Massachusetts. There was a girl I knew there who wasn't really a street person, but she hung with us when she came slumming. She called herself Elandra and she reminded me a lot of Stevie Nicks. She had the same hair, wore the same flowing gypsy witchy dresses. She was quite beautiful.

Somehow she had hooked up with a black hippie named T.C. and his old lady Libby. They were taking care of a farmhouse outside St. Johnsbury, Vermont, which was supposedly owned by the publisher of *The Village Voice*. Elandra said we should come up and visit, because they had only a couple of more weeks before the owner returned and their caretaking job would end. Mush, one of our tribe, said he had a friend in Plymouth, New Hampshire, that we could also visit, so we decided to head on up.

Surprisingly it didn't take me, Mush, and Lobo, another member of the tribe, long to hitch up to St. Johnsbury and find the farmhouse outside of town. T.C. and Libby were there, as well as Elandra and her boyfriend and a girl named Amanda. We spent a week hanging out at the farm, drinking and partying. The three of us competed with each other to get into Amanda's pants, but we had no luck. At the end of our stay T.C. said he was going to go up to Earth People Park. There was supposed to be a large party there for the Solstice, which was a few weeks away.

The Summer Solstice was when everybody on the street got together and raised hell. In the summers, the big events for all the Tribes wandering in America were either the Gathering of the Tribes every Fourth of July, or the Summer Solstice at Earth People's Park in June. The first Tribal Gathering had been at Strawberry Lake in Colorado in 1972. The 1973 Gathering was in the Wind River Wilderness Area in Wyoming. We couldn't make that, so we decided to go up to Earth People's Park for the Solstice.

But, that was a few weeks away, so we decided to head back down to Cambridge until then. On our way back to Cambridge we stopped in Plymouth and looked up Mush's friend. His name was Barry. Like Mush, he was also from New York. He was black and had a short Afro. We already knew someone named Barry, so we began calling the new Barry, "Blackberry."

The second night we were there we went over to some girl's house and the four of us and three girls who were there started drinking and getting high. Then the girls wanted us to take them to the local graveyard. It was allegedly haunted, so they were always afraid to go there at night by themselves.

So, we left their house and walked to the outer edges of Plymouth and found the cemetery. There was a large gate leading into the grounds. There was a fog hovering a few feet off the ground and it seemed like the temperature dropped as soon as we entered the gate. We wandered amongst the tombstones, fueling each other's paranoia in our stoned state. Then we began to hear strange things and noticed shapes moving throughout the fog.

Suddenly there was a loud shriek, whether it came from the girls or something else I didn't know. All I knew was that we all immediately turned and ran back to the entrance of the cemetery, trying not to trip over tombstones buried under the fog, the girls screaming all the way. We made it to the street and we stood there panting.

"Let's go back in", I whispered. Being used to spending nights wandering though cemeteries I was quite curious to check it out.

"Fuck that", one of the girls replied. "I'm out of here."

Since I couldn't convince anyone else to go back inside, and the girls were too scared to walk home alone, we left the Plymouth cemetery ghosts to rest in peace.

The next day we decided to head out. Blackberry said he would like to go with us to EPP for Solstice. so we made a plan to stop back there when we headed up to the Park.

The first night back in the Square, Super and Mugsy came in from Watertown. These were two local sisters who we met when Lobo first started hanging with me. We sort of adopted them as little sisters and protected them anytime they came into the Square. They were probably closer to our age than we imagined. I think Lobo secretly had a crush on Super, and she on Lobo, but neither ever acted on it.

One of the guys hanging out in the Square was named Funky Phil. He normally had a hitching partner named Dusty, who was somewhere else at the moment. He also wanted to go with us to EPP for the Solstice. Lobo and Mush and I talked about it and we decided that the odds of four guys getting rides together was long, so we decided that Lobo and Mush would hitch together and Phil would come with me.

Lobo's birthday was on June 14th and mine was the 17th so we decided to stay in Cambridge and celebrate there and then head up to the Park. Super made us a cake when the time came and we all sat in Harvard's Holyoke Center, the little park just adjacent to the Square, sharing cake, drinking whiskey and, as usual, generally making a huge nuisance of ourselves. We didn't start any fights with the citizens that night and, all and all, had a great birthday celebration.

We headed out the next day. Funky Phil liked his wine, so before leaving we bummed up enough in the Square for a couple of bottles of rotgut and headed north. I found out from Phil that he was a huge fan of *The Wizard of Oz*, so throughout our journey to the park we kept drinking and singing the whole catalog of songs from the movie. We got some strange looks from our rides as we sat in the back seat, sipping wine and singing, "Ha, ha, ha, ho, ho, ho, and a couple of tra la las, that's how we laugh the day away in the merry ol' Land of Oz." In a way, we were on our own journey to the Land of Oz.

We made it to the Park the next day. At that time the entrance was at a small house close to the highway. Some people stayed there. It was a long walk to get to the main part of the Park, skirting the edge of a neighboring farm. We all met up at the house and hung there most of the first day, drinking and bullshitting. We found out T.C. and Libby had split up and T.C. was with a woman named Denise in an A-frame up a trail we called Rabbit Alley. It was named that mainly because the trail meandered up to the Canadian border where American draft dodgers could cross over.

The Coaticook River ran through the Park and there was a homemade sauna on its bank. You could steam yourself and then run out and jump in the river. Despite the leeches and black flies, this was quite satisfying when it was 95 degrees and 100 percent humidity. There was also a large area where trees had been cut down that we called Stump Meadow. A lot of impromptu music jams were done there and it was where most everybody hung out on the Solstice.

When we got to the Park proper it was like some rendezvous of old-time Mountain Men. People who hadn't seen each other all year were slapping each other on the back. We were a rowdy bunch, dressed in leather with necklaces of teeth and feathers. We were twentieth century barbarians who loved to drink and loved to fight. All the women were from the streets and just as rowdy as the men. All we did was party and fuck. Sex was commonplace, and lots of times we'd fuck in front of others. Me and Lobo and T.C. had pussy eating contests with our women to see who could make them come first. I usually earned the title of The Fastest Tongue in the East.

Outsiders said we had no morals, but we had our own codes. When we drank, the first one to pass out got pissed on by everybody else, and many a night we all passed out together to avoid that fate. If we fought among ourselves, no one would jump in to help another if it was a fair fight. But, under no condition could you stand by and watch a brother get his ass kicked by a stranger. Against a common enemy most of us would have died for each other. All money was pooled and shared communally.

We always poured the first drink out of a whiskey bottle onto the earth in memory of our dead brothers -- who were getting to be numerous. A trunk ran over Dusty, Funky Phil's partner, while he was traveling to that summer's giant rock concert at Watkins Glen. The cops were always offing others, like Deputy Dawg. ODs claimed others.

The Park was home to a lot of colorful characters. The local guru, of sorts, was an older man named Brother

John. He had a spot where he hung out and ruminated with a lot of witticisms on philosophy. I liked him a lot and ended up spending many an hour discussing the world with him.

Michael Dodge was a friendly older guy who played some decent music and would join us many a time to play with us. There was a couple, Tom and Linda, who had a large house off the beaten path. He actually had a full sized piano and a couple of horses. I spent more than a few days at their house banging on the piano and hanging out.

Another couple I got to know well was Brad and Diane. They lived off the edge of the large meadow as you entered the Park proper. They had an amazing teepee that you couldn't see from the meadow. It was quite large, with a soft, carpeted floor surrounding a fire pit in the center of the teepee. Brad and I spent many an hour discussing Native American spirituality. Two of my favorite books that I carried in my backpack, along with my tattered copies of the Lord of the Rings trilogy, were John Fire Lamedeer's *Seeker of Visions* and *Black Elk Speaks*.

One night I went down to the Welcome Wagon where everybody was supposed to check his or her weapons. The Hog Farmers established an old hay wagon as the Welcome Wagon to pacify the cops, so they'd stop coming into the Park and raising hell. Seems Jim, a guy we knew, had gotten into a drunken argument with his partner over where to pitch their tent. Jim guy pulled a knife on his partner, just to scare him, and accidentally stabbed him in the kidneys and killed him. Jim was arrested and was down in the St. Johnsbury jail awaiting his trial. So the Welcome Wagon was established to pacify the heat. Everybody except *us* checked their weapons then they entered the Park.

Everybody had to pull shifts of guard duty on the Wagon, to make incoming people drop their weapons. This night I went down with a guitar I borrowed from someone. That's where I met Abbe. She was short, slim, and cute; she had long brown hair, and wore a ring in her nose long before that became the style. It was more than the ring in her nose that hooked me, though. She was there at the Welcome Wagon with her guitar, so we began playing together. After that, several of us walked back toward Crazy Al's cabin, a big A-frame towards the back of the Park that Abbe lived in. He was really burned out, which was why we all called him "Crazy Al." It was near the A-frame where I was crashing, so I had an excuse to walk with her.

On the way Abbe slipped and fell in a big mud puddle. I helped her up. We laughed our asses off. We were both totally drunk. We got to Crazy Al's and Abbe took some downers and we sat around laughing, and the next thing I knew we were fucking. The next morning she moved into my A-frame with me. We got along nicely and loved to play and sing together. Abbe and I also fucked a lot, so I really began to like her, and I thought it'd be nice to have a steady woman for a while.

Abbe and I sang together in Stump Meadow quite often. She was a great singer and I loved listening to her. I had this crude little ditty based on a Stephen Foster minstrel song that I sang at times, usually when I was inebriated: "Suck on her cunt 'til her head caves in, do-da, do-da, suck on her cunt all the do-da day."

Then Abbe would sing, "Rolly Poly, tickle my holy, eat my slimy slew, drag my balls across the halls and eat my asshole too." We got along great and I was soon crazy about her.

We had a friend named H. B. who was having a birthday party about a week or so later, on the Fourth of July, so a lot of us went to his cabin in the woods. One of the guys, Craig, had a car, so we were thinking of piling in it and heading back to Berkeley after the party. Abbe, though, decided not to go to H.B.'s party, because she didn't want to go back to Berkeley. She said she had to go down to New York City, instead. I'd never spent a lot of time with a woman before this. The longest had been with Tula in Taos. When Tula decided to go back to Taste, it hit me pretty hard. Now, it seemed Abbe might be leaving. I had strong feelings for Abbe, but it looked like we were splitting up.

Anyway, the rest of us piled into Craig's car for H.B.'s party at his cabin outside of Bellows Falls, Vermont. A lot of the STP Family hung out there. Two guys sniffing Sterno carried around this little guy named Midget Jessie, who had two crippled legs. He had a little shed about as big as a closet and he'd just sit in there with his can of Sterno, sniffing it.

I'd met Midget Jessie earlier down in Cambridge. He was sitting in Harvard Square's Holyoke Center with his crippled legs and five quarts of beer. People passing by would ask for a drink and he'd break his bottle and try to cut'em up. He'd grab up handfuls of glass and throw it at them, cutting his hands to ribbons. Then he'd hobble after them on his crippled legs trying to cut them with his broken bottle.

While we were at H.B.'s cabin we raided the town of Bellows Falls and raised hell all the time. The good citizens called the cops to kick us out of the cabin, so we decided to go back to Berkeley to escape the harassment. This was Lobo, me, T.C. and his old lady, and Craig. Abbe decided to stay at Earth People's Park. Craig had a car. We didn't have any money, but we had Craig's car. And we had a hose. So, we five siphoned our way across New York state and on across Ohio and into Michigan. There we decided to drop in on Ann Arbor, another gathering place of the Tribes.

The first night we were in Ann Arbor someone gave us some acid. We took it and then ran all over town acting like crazies. We were the only weirdoes in leather-patched pants carrying knives at our sides screaming up and down the streets of Ann Arbor. I also had the dead feet of a muskrat I'd found by the side of the road hanging from my belt. They stunk highly. For some reason, we immediately attracted the attention of the cops. So, we retreated to a commune-like mansion on the edge of the university campus in a neighborhood called University Village or Village Corner, something like that.

This 300-lb. girl was already crashing there, and she instantly fell in love with Lobo because of his blond hair. She was trying harder than hell to get Lobo to fuck her. She was about ready to rape him and he was trying to keep her away. So, I figured I'd leave them to their dance and go drive Craig's car around town and maybe pick up some women. I was wearing no shoes and no shirt, just a Levi vest and my leather pants. I drove around the block, and as soon as I did there was this cop behind me. Pulled me over.

"Where's your license?"

"Hell, I ain't got one."

"Where's your registration?"

"I don't know."

"Whose car is this?"

"A friend of mine's."

"What's his name?"

"Craig."

"Craig what?"

"I don't know."

"Get out of the car, boy. What're you doing with that knife on your side? That's a concealed weapon! You're under arrest!"

So, I'm in the Ann Arbor jail. The first thing the cops did was take out a can of Lysol and spray me down. I was grungy-looking. My pants could stand in a corner by themselves. When they emptied my pockets they found all these medicine bags filled with teeth and beads and bones. They didn't know what to make of them. Then they threw me into this tiny 6' x 8' cell in the bottom of the jail. It had a cross grate in the middle of the floor for the toilet, a cement block to sleep on, and was reached by three electronic doors.

By the next night I was getting pretty pissed off because they wouldn't let me make a phone call, so nobody knew where the hell I was. Then I heard the three electronic doors: *Unnnnnahhh, clang! Unnnnnahhh, clang! Unnnnnahhh, clang!* Here came Lobo, T.C., and *Bernie,* who I hadn't seen since Taos! He'd been to the Gathering of the Tribes in Wyoming and was heading up to Earth People's Park. He just happened to stop in Ann Arbor, and met up with Lobo. I shouted out our special yell in great joy, and we all hugged.

I asked how was it they all came to visit me, and it seems they were drinking, of course. They'd found out from rumors on the street that I was in jail; someone had seen me get busted. They'd been going around with a "Morgan Defcnsc Fund" box collecting bail money. But, all the money they collected they used to get drunk on. They ran out of money, so they went into a liquor store and T.C. tried to steal a bottle of Jack Daniels. He wasn't very good at shoplifting, or maybe the clerks just watched him closer because he was black, so, of course, he was caught. Three clean-cut college students grabbed him and stuffed him in the basement until the cops came.

But, T.C. had this two and a half-pound sledgehammer he called "Thunderfuck" that he always carried at his side. He grabbed Thunderfuck and started smashing his way out of the basement. The three college kids jumped on him, so Bernie and Lobo jumped on them. They tore the store apart. Put nine people in the hospital.

So, there were now four of us in this dinky little cell about as big as a bed. It was crowded as hell, like the Black Hole of Calcutta. The cops came down and sprayed us with Raid and Lysol all the time. Meanwhile, we were all dying for a cigarette. We kept bugging this big black guard for a cigarette. He just gave us grief. So, we decided that the next time he came around, we'd all pick off a louse -- we all had lice -- and we'd threaten to throw them on him if he didn't give us a cigarette.

He came down and I called out, "Hey! C'mere, quick! It's an emergency!" He came over and I held up a louse between my thumb and finger. "See this? We're all gonna throw these in your hair if you don't give us a cigarette! You'll have a hell of a time explaining the lice to your old lady!" He gave each of us a cigarette.

For a toilet, as I said, all we had was this shithole in the middle of the floor. To make it even more complicated, it had a cross grate, so you had to shit between the bars. But they wouldn't give us toilet paper. We'd been in there for a couple of days, but we couldn't shit because we didn't have any toilet paper. They also wouldn't flush the thing whenever we pissed. They had to flush it for us, and refused to do it. They said we animals would feel more at home with the stink. We decided we had to protest these conditions.

So, at dinner time they gave us our food, and then each of us shit in our empty plate and gave it back to the guard. They started screaming at us. We started screaming back, "Give us some toilet paper, or we're gonna shit in your plates every fucking day!"

"Well, you guys just won't eat!"

"Then we'll eat our fucking lice, we don't care!"

Ten minutes later the toilet flushed for the first time. Five minutes after that they threw us a roll of toilet paper for the first time.

I spent twelve days in that tiny Ann Arbor cell. One day the other three were taken away and they never came back. I figured they'd been released, and was pleased for them, but I also felt wronged.

They were free after smashing up a liquor store, while I was still in jail for some stupid charge! Finally, I was taken to court. I had this lawyer that the fat girl who was in love with Lobo provided. As we were going up to the court in the elevator together he said that if I pleaded "no contest" to disorderly conduct, I'd be sentenced to time served. That sounded fine to me.

Unbeknownst to me, Abbe, Laura, and Beverly arrived in Ann Arbor from the Park while I was in jail. Beverly was 4' 11," her two front teeth were missing, and she was nuts. They'd decided to head for Berkeley, just as we'd been, and had stopped in Ann Arbor and run into Lobo and the others. So the whole front row of spectator seating in the courtroom was filled with Lobo, black T.C. looking fierce in his black beret, Bernie in his home-made buckskin jacket with rabbit legs hanging from it, and the three girls. As soon as I walked in everybody cheered and Laura and Beverly and Abbe grabbed their tits and started shaking them, yelling, "Suck my tit! Suck my tit!"

We did things like that all the time just to cause a stir. Once, out on the Ann Arbor streets after I was released, we all got drunk and Abbe was rubbing my balls. She unzipped my pants and started playing with my dick. The next thing I knew she was down on her knees giving me a blowjob right there in public with people walking by. After that I'd be sitting on a garbage can and she'd be blowing me while I hit up people walking by for spare change. It was just a way of freaking them out.

Anyway, the judge pounded his gavel and yelled, "Order in the court! Order in the court!" Then he turned to me and asked me how I pled to the charge of disorderly conduct.

"No contest," I said.

"Do you understand what that means?"

"Yes, sir, it means I'm not guilty, but I don't want to sit in jail for six months to prove I'm not guilty." The lawyer elbowed me.

The judge said, "That's not quite right." But, he gave me time served, told me to get out of town within 48 hours, and, bang! I'm outta there! The first thing I did was go with the gang and eat a good steak. Then Abbe and me and the tribe returned to this abandoned 30-room mansion on Hill Street where the 300-lb. girl lived. There were now about 35 of us crashing there. Then I took a good shit where I could wipe my ass.

My very first night out of jail we went back to the liquor store T.C. and company had busted up. For some reason, they'd dropped the charges against him. I think it was because they couldn't prove he was shoplifting and T.C. said they assaulted him first.

So, we were panhandling in front of this liquor store, saying things like, "I need some tennis shoes for my armadillo," whatever. General bullshit lines.

Some hulking giant of a clean-cut football player came by. I hit him up for spare change and he said, "Fuck you!"

I let it slide, but T.C. was in a foul mood. He yelled, "What'd you say to my brother, you muttha fucker?" He attacked the guy and the giant started beating the shit out of him. He got T.C. down and had his head on the curbstone, banging it against the pavement. I ran up and kicked the jock in the face.

This got him off T.C. and he started messing with me. Then I saw T.C. coming up behind him with a big board with a nail in it. Someone yelled, "Look out!" T.C. swung and got the jock in the elbow. The nail went deep into his arm. Blood spurted when T.C. jerked it out, and the jock started yelling, "Put that down and fight like a man!"

T.C. said, "OK, I'll put it down," and dropped the board. Then he jerked a bottle out of the mouth of some rubbernecking dude, broke the bottle, and tried to cut the jock's face. The jock started screaming, "Save me! Help me!" Meanwhile, his arm was gushing blood.

I grabbed T.C. and pulled him across the road. We got about a block away when the cops stopped us. They all knew me from my time in jail. "It's Morgan M. Morgan, the sonuvabitch." The jock had disappeared, so they told me I had one more night to get out of town.

We all booked back to the mansion. There we got drunk, raised hell, and went to this concert. Lobo brought along this new girl that he was sleeping with who'd just come in from Earth People's Park with a huge stash of mescaline. I was wearing Bernie's buckskin shirt with the fringe. We got into the concert for free and started flipping out from the mesc. I was dancing all over like mad. Someone gave me a tambourine and I jumped up on stage and began banging the tambourine.

After we got back to the mansion, the cops raided the place. We climbed onto the roof and sat up there polishing off our wine while the cops dragged off a lot of the others. After the cops left, we climbed down, drank some more, fucked, and went to sleep.

The next morning we decided to go to Watkins Glen, in upstate New York's Finger Lake District, where the Grateful Dead, the Allman Brothers, and The Band were going to headline what was supposed to be the biggest rock concert of all time, bigger than Woodstock. So, we split into different groups. Lobo, T.C., and T.C.'s old lady hitchhiked straight to Watkins Glen. Turned out it *was* bigger than Woodstock. On July 29th half-a-million freaks -- 95 acres of wall-to-wall people -- jammed into a Grand Prix racetrack for 12 hours of non-stop music. It created a bigger traffic jam than Woodstock, with thousands walking in from as far as 30-miles out after the roads were clotted with an endless sea of abandoned cars. The only reason the Watkins Glen concert isn't as well known as Woodstock is because Woodstock came first, and Joni Mitchell didn't write a song about it.

Meanwhile, Abbe and me and a black guy named Otis decided to hitch back to Earth People's Park and catch a ride with the Hog Farmers to Watkins Glen. The Hog Farm had to clean up the Park in order to somehow pay that year's property tax, so we were going back to help. We got to the Park and helped clean up, but then the fucking Hog Farmers wouldn't let us on their bus to Watkins Glen. I guess they considered us the scourge of Earth People's Park, and they didn't want us along.

These Hog Farmers were *constantly* on our case. These were the so-called "super cool hippies." They handled the O.D. clinic at Woodstock, those things. They had Wavy Gravy singing his fucking weirdo songs. The last time I saw Wavy Gravy he was sitting in a corner with a one-string guitar going *boing, boing, boing*.

But the people at Earth People's Park weren't just the Hog Farmers. Those guys were a minority. And it was the *people* from Earth People's Park who made $21,000 picking up the trash at Watkins Glen. This money was supposed to pay property taxes on the Park, but the Hog Farmers took the money and went to Switzerland.

So, the fucking Hog Farmers took off for Watkins Glen, leaving Abbe and me behind. The roads around Watkins Glen had been closed off, so we couldn't even hitchhike there. We had to stay at the Park while Lobo got to attend the biggest rock concert in history! I was ready to shoot some Hog Farmers, but I didn't have a gun.

After the Hog Farmers left for the concert, there were some other abandoned people around the Park, but mostly it was just me and Abbe, so we fucked a lot. About two or three days later I went to the Park's Post Office box in Norton, the nearest town, and found about $300 in food stamps. Hippies would come up from Boston and sign up for welfare and food stamps and everybody used the same P. O. box. After those hippies left, food stamps kept coming to the P. O. box. Whoever needed them, took them. So, I cashed them. There was a store in Norton that let you buy anything with food stamps: Socks, underwear, whiskey, whatever you wanted. I stocked up with all kinds of goodies for those of us the fucking Hog Farmers left behind.

Then I stumbled on a 45-ton stash of Jimson Weed at the Park, which is the strongest hallucinogenic in the world. A lot of people on acid say they hallucinate, but most of the time they just see the real world a little distorted. But Jimson Weed, I soon discovered, put you into a whole different world. It's also highly poisonous.

It's a form of belladonna. *It's a weed!* I stuffed a coffee pot *full* of the stuff. Brewed it for eight hours. Poured it as thick as syrup into a cup. Drank it. It was the most putrid shit I've ever tasted. It was like you took a lot of dead bodies and squeezed'em into juice and drank it.

After drinking it I climbed up into the loft of the A-frame and lay down. About fifteen minutes later I was thirsty as hell. I tried to get up, but my body had turned into two tons of lead, so I couldn't move. Now, the rest of this I hallucinated. According to the people around me, I stood in one spot for twelve hours. According to *me*, I was *every place!* I was horseback riding in the Rocky Mountains, dodging diesel trucks, talking to raccoons, dodging silkworms trying to lasso me.

Next thing I know, I'm inside the A-frame again. I'm lying in the bed and three dwarfs wearing pointed hats of different colors were sitting at the foot of the bed. For hours they sat there, never saying a word, just nodding their heads. Then people came up and started talking to me. My grandfather came up and spoke to me.

My brother, Eric, was there, and spoke to me. Thousands of people from my whole life came up and spoke to me. The dwarfs nodded at everything they said. It was a psychedelic "This Is Your Life!" At some point I fell asleep and woke up in the loft late the next afternoon.

I decided this was neat stuff and proceeded to turn other people on to it. I became a *brujo*. That's what Mexicans call a Medicine Man, Witch Doctor, whatever, brewing up doses for people. I gave it to this ridge-runner from North Carolina. He disappeared for three days. We looked *everywhere* for him. On the third day we found him naked, hugging a tree. He said it was his wife and he wouldn't leave her, because it was their honeymoon. So, we left someone there to watch over him.

For about a week there'd also been this fifty-year old man strolling past Earth People's Park. He was always asking for acid, grass, whatever. Turned out he was the engineer of the train which ran between nearby Island Pond -- Island Puddle, we called it -- and Canada. He'd gotten into a fight with his wife, derailed the train, and had been given a leave of absence to recuperate. So, he came to Earth People's Park to trip out and get high, and he ran into me. I gave him some Jimson Weed. He drank about three glasses, went into the A-frame and fell asleep.

I stayed up all that night counting heads, checking on everybody I'd given Jimson Weed to. If I was giving this shit to people, I should at least watch over them. One guy was out in the middle of the woods picking up tiny twigs for hours and hours in the middle of the night. I said, "What're you doing?"

"I'm getting my winter firewood." Then he reached over and closed an imaginary window and complained that it was awfully cold.

About five or six in the morning, just as I was starting to doze off, the engineer jumped up, looked at his watch, and cried, "My God! I'm late for work!"

I thought he was OK, but then he ran out into the yard, stripped off his clothes, and ran into the woods. We chased him, but he disappeared. We finally heard that he was found in Canaan, eighteen miles away, babbling like an idiot and walking the streets naked. Luckily, he was too far gone to tell anyone he came from Earth People's Park, or we'd have been hanged. But, I think it ruined his career as an engineer.

I did this stuff three times, the only one who did it that much. It was beginning to affect me physically. I started going blind. I couldn't walk. I had no muscle control. That's when I read up on it and discovered *it was poisonous*. The reason there aren't any belladonna addicts is because they all die before they become addicted to it. I figured it was time to lay off that shit.

One day Kenny Redport and Asshole Dave, two STPers, showed up. They crashed in the A-frame and that night Bernie got into a fight with Asshole Dave. Seems Bernie had caught a small cat that was wandering around the Park, killed it, and ate it. We had plenty of food, but Bernie just wanted to see what cat meat tasted like. The cat turned out to be the kitten of some chick, and when she saw the skin she flipped out. That night Asshole Dave and Bernie got into a fight over the cat. This created a hostility between them that went on for a long time.

Meanwhile, Abbe and me were having difficulties. When we weren't fucking, we were arguing. The same night that Bernie and Asshole Dave fought over the cat, Abbe said she was tired of everyone fighting. She said we should all get the fuck out of the A-frame, because the guy who'd built it had said she could have it when he left the Park.

She was also in a general bitchy mood because she was pregnant. I wasn't sure if it was my kid, because everyone fucked everyone. I couldn't put up with her moods, so I told her she could have the A-frame and I moved into the teepee across the trail, which belonged to a guy named Derrick and his wife.

Meanwhile, Lobo and T.C. and T.C.'s old lady stayed in Watkins Glen for two weeks cleaning up 90 tons of garbage and eating pickled squash, all courtesy of the Hog Farm. Eventually, about the middle of August, everybody came back. They brought all kinds of stuff with them that people had abandoned: A whole truckload of brand new sleeping bags, tents, all kinds of dope. Lobo also found me a new guitar that someone had abandoned, to replace the one Taste smashed over the cop's head in Albuquerque. That night we had a big party and our own concert.

But, there was a narc in Paradise. There were narcs at Earth People's Park all the time. This one came in a school bus with his supposed wife. Everybody knew he was a Fed -- he kept running around taking pictures of everybody -- but no one wanted to do anything about him. So, we in the STP Family did. We tried to set fire to the school bus. We broke the windows and tossed in kerosene, followed by matches. Unfortunately, it didn't catch.

He lodged a complaint with the Hog Farmers. They called a big meeting of the entire Park to discuss this incident, which we refused to attend. Since we wouldn't go to the Hog Farmers, they moved the meeting to us. The whole Park, led by the

Hog Farmers, paraded into our front yard. They got on us for trashing this guy's school bus. We told'em we'd blow the school bus up if the Fed didn't leave. David, the leader of the Hog Farmers, and me got into a big shouting argument.

Meanwhile, all the other Hog Farmers were sitting around going, "Ommmm! Ommmm! Ommmm!" They "Ommmmed" every time they had a problem. The zucchini wasn't cooked right, so "Ommmm!" Before they sat down to eat, "Ommmm!" As they fucked, "Ommmm!" Taking a shit, "Ommmm!" I'm getting ready to punch this asshole out, and these bees are buzzing all around!

So, we STPers started chanting, "Ommmm, Mother Fuckerrrr! Ommmm, Mother Fuckerrrr!" That really pissed them off.

Then we just told'em to drag their fucking vegetarian asses out of our front yard, or we'd stick their corn cobs up their asses. This pissed them off some more, and they stopped Ommmming and ran off to get their guns.

So, we got *our* guns. We sat at the windows of the A-frame with our guns and were going to blow their fucking heads off when they came back. We were prepared for a Big Hippie Massacre at Earth People's Park. But then Kirk, the Park's Dope Commissioner, settled things. He convinced the Hog Farmers to not come back, although *we* wanted them to. He persuaded them that they'd all go to that Great Cabbage Patch in the Sky if they came back, which was true. After that, the Hog Farmers decided to abandon Earth People's Park. Once they left, the Park essentially belonged to us in the STP Family and miscellaneous hippies.

After the face-off with the Hog Farmers we decided to go to Max's Party. This was a once-a-year event held in early September at some guy's place near Newport, not far from Earth People's Park. He had live bands, beer, everything, all in a big field. But this year Max, the "Super Cool Hippie," decided to charge admission. To collect the money and protect his property he decided to copy the Stones at Altamont, when they hired the

Hell's Angels to provide security, and so he hired a biker gang called The Drifters. People began harassing the bikers, so the bikers pulled out shotguns and started shooting. They wounded seven people. Max then decided to throw open the gates. The bikers didn't like that and continued to beat people up.

Anyway, we got to the front of the stage and hung our STP flag on the edge of the stage. There were maybe 40 of us, including Slim, Phineas T. Wabbit, Israel, and a lot of others. The Family chose me to be thrown up on the stage, grab the mike, and start a revolution against the bikers. So, they threw me up on stage, I grabbed the mike, and I started rallying people to fight the bikers. Instantly, about ten bikers threw me back into the crowd. We decided to raise hell with the bikers later on.

The bands came on, played for about an hour, and then decided the vibes were getting crazy, so they left. So, you had thousands of disappointed people, hundreds of crazy and homicidal bikers, a bunch of angry STPers -- and no fucking music! So, *we* STPers took over the stage. We leapt around, clanking bottles together, screaming and yelling. We did this all night.

The next morning there were some river rats hanging around. "River rats" were local yokels, young kids, 14 or 15, who gravitated to us when we went from town to town, and we let'em hang around. Most of us weren't all that much older. Lobo had just turned 17 and I'd just turned 18, but we seemed a lot older. Anyway, about 15 bikers were beating on these two river rats, so we intervened. There were six of us: Me, Stinkin' Lincoln, H.B., Israel, Slim, and Phineas T. Wabbit. We told the bikers to back off.

So, they proceeded to beat the shit out of us. I was fighting two and a half bikers. One was a skinny black dude that I didn't have any problem with. The other was a 300-lb. berserker. I smashed his nose with my fist as hard as I could, and it splattered all over his face. He just laughed. I figured that was the end of me. Next thing I knew he was sitting on top of me. He kept beating me in the face with a cast on his arm, which is how my front teeth came to be chipped. It was just: *Smash! Smash! Smash!*

Two hours later I woke up under the stage, dried blood all over me. I chugged a couple of shots of whiskey, went to the medical station, and got patched up.

That night everybody continued to party. I was very drunk and was stumbling back toward our car when I came upon Wabbit and some others just standing around. I saw Abbe on the ground, crying, and this fucking biker on top of her. He'd ripped her blouse off. I couldn't figure out what was happening. Here was my old lady on the ground with an ape on top of her, and my brothers were just standing there! I was confused and looked around for a minute or so until I realized the biker wasn't fucking around. This was for real! He was trying to rape her! So, I walked up to him and kicked him in the teeth as hard as I could.

The rest of the story was told to me later, because I don't remember any of it. I didn't get the details until two years later, because I didn't see any of my people right after that. There were three bikers and one pulled out a .45 and told everybody to sit down. Another grabbed an axe handle and another had a lead pipe and they proceeded to play bongos on my head. I don't even remember getting hit the first time. They kept beating on me even after I was out cold. I was told that Wabbit finally jumped in and also got his head busted. I vaguely remember being on the ground with Abbe screaming next to me. Eventually, they left me for dead. I remember being in an ambulance. I remember waking up in the Newport hospital with a terrible headache. I didn't know why I was in the hospital. Had I passed out drunk under the stage and suffocated? What?

I remember the doctors arguing over who was going to treat this worthless hunk of meat. Two days had passed and the doctors still couldn't decide who was going to touch me. They hadn't done any X-rays, hadn't cleaned off the dried blood, and hadn't even taken off my clothes. I was lying in the hospital bed in my filthy blood clotted clothes! Some friends, Brad and Diane, came to visit and I asked them if they had a car. They said they did, so I pulled the IVs out of my arm, threw them on the floor, walked out of the hospital, and we drove back to Earth People's Park.

While I was laying in the hospital in a coma with the doctors arguing over who was going to touch me, T.C., Lobo, and Bernie got drunk and wandered into downtown Newport. There, T.C. and Bernie got into a fight with each other, because they never got along too well. As they were fighting, a woman came by pushing a baby stroller. T.C. grabbed it and threw it at Bernie. Luckily, there was no baby in it, but the lady screamed for the cops.

The cops appeared and began beating the shit out of T.C., so Lobo jumped in. He kicked a cop in the ribs and broke his ribs. Eventually, the cops handcuffed them all and they were thrown into a cop car, which didn't have a screen between the driver and the prisoners in the back seat. Since they figured they were going to catch hell for fighting cops anyway, and had nothing to lose, all three began kicking the cop driving in the back of the head. The other cop turned around and began hitting their legs with his club, so they began kicking him, too. Somehow Bernie and T.C., who started it all, were released after a few days, while Lobo was sentenced to 60 days in jail. I didn't know this at the time. I heard about it once I got back to the Park.

The night I got back I began having horrible headaches. I couldn't remember anything. I had terrible pains in my head, and also my neck, because it seems I'd been clobbered in the neck also. I started hallucinating. A hunchbacked dwarf named Quasimodo came and talked to me. I crawled around in the fields on my hands and knees for hours talking to him. He'd lead me here and there in hide and seek. I'd scream weird battle cries. This can be verified by anyone who was there.

I then moved out of the teepee and back into the A-frame with Abbe. After the run-in with the bikers, she'd gone down to New York City to see her mother. She was gone for a while. When she came back she told me she wasn't pregnant any more.

One day we went into Newport to get food stamps and to see about me getting some free glasses. My glasses had been smashed in the battle with the bikers and I couldn't see worth shit. I went to the welfare office to apply for them. This old lady I spoke to turned me down. I asked why. She said, "Because."

"That's not a good enough reason," I said. I told her I was ill. What did I have to do to prove it? Did I have to tear her office apart?

"You can just go right ahead," she sniffed.

So I did. I stood up and tipped over her desk and knocked over the dividers to her cubicle. I grabbed the American flag in the corner and broke the staff over my knee. Then I went into the waiting room, sat down, and refused to leave.

They called the cops. When the cops came, I told them I wasn't going to leave. I said I'd just gotten out of the hospital with a head injury, and if they tried to force me to leave, I'd fight, and if they hit me over the head they'd kill me and *somebody* would sue them!

Meanwhile, the old lady was having a heart attack and screaming. The director called an emergency meeting and I walked out with food stamps, about $18 in cash for medical supplies, and an appointment to get an eye exam for free eyeglasses, which I later got.

At some point we decided to visit H.B. in some small southern Vermont hamlet. We stopped in St. Johnsbury to visit Lobo, who was still serving his 60 days in the local jail. We all crashed at an apartment belonging to Moe, T.C.'s old lady at the time. Amazon Brenda from the Park was there. She was big-boned, a six-foot giant, could rape anybody she liked. There was also a little Puerto Rican dude I'd never seen before named Juan Valez. He ran around screaming, "My father led the Revolution!" I don't know what Puerto Rican revolution he was referring to, but his father led it. There were also three river rats from Connecticut.

Abbe was also there, and Beverly with the missing front teeth. While Abbe was in New York City seeing her mom, I'd been fucking Beverly for a while. She'd been in the loft of the A-frame one day and yelled down, "Who wants to eat my pussy?"

"I'll eat your pussy," I yelled back, and did so, and then we fucked. This was no problem for Abbe, as everything was communal.

Well, of course we all wanted to party, even though it was the middle of the night. Unfortunately, none of us had any money. As luck would have it, this apartment was above a combination liquor and grocery store, which I decided to burglarize. I went down and picked the lock on the back window and climbed in. I went to the freezer and pulled out some cases of beer and some wine and went back up. I wiped off everything I touched and put the lock back on the window when I left.

We all got stinking drunk. It was the first time I'd gotten drunk since Max's Party. I ambled off to take a bath with Abbe. We sat in the bathtub drinking wine and getting even more drunk. Amazon

Brenda was nude and in the corner fucking herself with a cucumber to freak out the three river rats. She was calling all the men sexless wimps because no one would fuck her. Beverly was running around nude screaming, "Somebody eat my pussy! Who wants to eat my pussy?"

I finally climbed out of the tub and sat down on a chair. I began to doze off because I was really drunk. Suddenly there were three fur burgers staring me in the face. It was Abbe, Beverly, and Amazon Brenda. Since I had a reputation as a great pussy-eater, they were all competing to see whose pussy I was going to eat first. I didn't need this, as I was feeling very ill from too much wine, and the sight of these three pussies in my face was not particularly appealing. I just let'em fight it out and fell asleep.

About six in the morning I woke up to the smell of hamburger. I walked into the kitchen and found pounds and pounds of hamburger all over the place. Seems the three river rats from Connecticut had been inspired by my acquisition of liquor and went down to the store for food. But, not only did they leave the window wide open, it was now daylight and people saw the stupid fucks!

Someone yelled that there was an army of cops forming up outside. We all started running around trying to get rid of the hamburger. Everybody was stuffing it in their mouths, flushing it down the toilet, throwing it out the windows, anything to get rid of all the pounds and pounds of hamburger!

T.C. jumped out the window and booked up the street. People disappeared to different places. Juan and me were the only guys left there with all the girls. The cops knocked on the door. I answered and kept the door shut as much as possible.

"Hello," they said. "We have a report of a disturbance up here." They tried to look over my shoulder into the apartment.

"No, officer," I said politely. "There's no disturbance up here."

"OK, just keep it down."

I closed the door and seconds later State Troopers kicked in the back door, the back windows, came through the front door. They had shotguns, rifles, and riot gear. "Get your ass up against the wall!" they yelled and threw us all up against it. Juan Valez cried, "Viva la revolution!" and attacked a sergeant, who threw him out the door and down the stairs. They pushed me out the door. They grabbed Amazon Brenda, who was still nude and flapping her tits at them. They gave her time to put on a dress, then they took us all to the St. Johnsbury police station.

They had all of us, including T.C., everyone, all lined up. Then Detective Shank, a baldheaded fucker about 50-years-old, walked in. He walked down the line from person to person. "Name? Age? Name? Age?" Right down the line. He got to Amazon Brenda. She lifted up her skirt and rubbed her nude pussy up against his leg and yelled in his face, "Fuck me! Fuck me!" Abbe and Beverly immediately flopped out their tits and started screaming, "Fuck me! Fuck me!" General chaos ensued as the three girls kept screaming, "Fuck me! Fuck me!" Shank was about ready to have a heart attack. He probably beat off to that memory for the next 40 years.

Anyway, the cops decided to arrest only me, Juan, T.C., and the three river rats, all for breaking and entering and grand larceny. Everyone else was released. Our loyal female comrades, including Abbe, immediately left town, not bothering to stick around to see what would happen to us. That's the last I saw of Abbe on the streets.

So, the six of us were sent to the local jail, which seemed to be a central holding pen for the entire area, because Lobo was there. Our friend Jim, from the Park, was there, too. He was the one who had accidentally stabbed his partner and killed him while arguing over where to put their tent at the Park. He'd been there for some time and was awaiting his trial. There were also several other street people that we knew from here and there who'd been picked up for this and that. So, it was a joyful reunion.

Nine days later we went to court on the charges. In the meantime, I volunteered for a lie detector test. I said I was in bed fucking Abbe the whole time, and I concentrated on the mental image of Amazon Brenda fucking herself with that cucumber. I passed with flying colors. There was no evidence against me.

Just before seeing the judge I was shown into this room to meet my court-appointed attorney. This ancient old dude must've been 90-years-old and greeted me in a croaking voice. He told me that if I pleaded guilty to petty larceny, I'd be sentenced to time served and I could leave. Otherwise, I'd have to sit in jail for six months in order for my case to come to trial. So, it seemed I'd be sentenced to six months for being innocent, or nine days for being guilty, so I decided to plead guilty.

In court the D.A. said to the judge, "Your Honor, we recommend that the charges be reduced to petty larceny and the defendant be sentenced to time served."

The judge nodded in seeming agreement and turned to me. "How do you plead to petty larceny?"

"Guilty, your Honor," I said.

The judge thought about it for a few minutes and then said. "Well, we can't let you young people get away with things like this. I sentence you all to 20 days in the St. Johnsbury Correctional Center."

So, T.C. and me and Juan and the river rats were sent back to join Lobo, and I was just pissed as hell at the whole set-up. Lobo and me proceeded to make ourselves royal nuisances to irritate the guards. We had total disdain for them. We banged on the bars all night chanting Indian songs. "Heyyy ya! Heyyy ya!" We did this all night. When the guards told me to shut up, I said, "Fuck you, this is my religion."

Now, I was wacky anyways, because I was still delusional from the beating the bikers gave me, but I decided to be even wackier. When the guards took me to the Visitor's Room, I wrapped my blanket around me and sat cross-legged on the table and chanted all night. "Heyyy ya! Heyyy ya!" Anytime the guards tried to come in, I picked up a chair and threw it at the fucking door. Around dawn they yelled in if I wanted some coffee. I was getting pretty tired, so I decided to call a truce. I gulped the coffee down and immediately keeled over. They'd drugged it. They dragged me back to my cell and left me there.

From then on we got revenge by using our spoons to flip gobs of peanut butter at them. We also stole Styrofoam cups from the coffee rack and at night we'd set'em on fire and throw them out into the hall until we had a big blaze going. Then we'd yell, "Fire! Fire!" They came running in with their fire extinguishers and we'd all be snoring in our bunks.

Next we organized the whole jail to participate in "Zoo Call." At midnight, every night, when things were nice and quite, the animals in the zoo went wild. Everybody began banging on the walls and howling like animals. I started out first howling like a wild monkey. "Ooh, ooh, ah, ah! Ooh, ooh, ah, ah!" Others were squealing like pigs, neighing like horses, mooing like cows. Lobo was going "ROAR! GROWL! SNARL!" He'd actually say the words, but he'd *roar* out the word, "roar"; he'd *growl* out the word "growl"; he'd *snarl* out the word "snarl."

As soon as the guards opened the door, everyone was snoring away peacefully in their bunks. *Everybody! Perfect* timing! The guards yelled, "You God-damned sonuvabitch! Go to sleep!" As soon as they shut the door, the zoo erupted again. We kept it up until dawn. The guards were so fucking pissed off they threatened to call the state riot police to haul us down to the state prison in Windsor.

So, we quieted down, because it was a pretty nice jail. This jail in St. Johnsbury was actually a large old house that had been converted into a jail with the cells in the main room. They had lots of fresh milk, Kool-Aid, coffee, bread and butter, peanut butter and jelly to make sandwiches, all available anytime you wanted. This was all in addition to your three square meals a day.

But, one night we had a confrontation with them over the late-night TV movie. It was Clint Eastwood's "The Good, the Bad, and the Ugly," which we all wanted to see. Now, we were supposed to get into our cells for lockdown at ten o'clock. When ten o'clock came around, we refused to move, because the movie hadn't ended. We were watching the movie and they yelled, "Lights out! Get in your cells!" We sat there, just watching the movie. "Get your asses in your cells!" We just sat there watching Clint Eastwood. The movie was about halfway through.

They turned the TV off. Nobody budged. We just sat there staring at the blank screen. They called for the captain and he sat there talking to us. "You know we'll have to call in the riot squad if you don't get into your cells," he said. Nobody said a word. We just kept staring at the blank screen. I'm talking about every damn prisoner, maybe 45 of us. Total silence.

After about 30-minutes the captain turned the TV back on and we finished watching "The Good, the Bad, and the Ugly." Then we turned off the TV and we all went to bed. That was the end of that.

After you were there about a week you were entitled to recreation privileges. This meant access to the rec room in the basement where they had the pool tables. So, all of us from the Park took over the room and ran out the local farm boys who were in for hitting a cop while they were drunk. "Hey, man!" they protested. "I'm in here for hitting a cop!"

"Yeah, well I'm in here for first degree murder."

"Oh, well, go ahead, man. Listen, you need someone to play with you sometime, I'll be over here in the corner...."

The guards asked us what we wanted for hobbies, so we told them we needed leather and needles. They gave it to us! So, we sat in there patching our leather pants with more leather. After that we called off the peanut butter shit.

Upstairs there was a small library with a table, some chairs, some cards and poker chips. We got tired of the rec room, so we took over the library. We sealed it off. No one could come in unless we let him in. We ran the whole fucking jail.

We'd sit up there and read what few books they had. We gave the farm boys the romances and the Ellery Queen novels; we kept the good stuff, the Conans, the Westerns, and the science fiction.

We also played poker all the time for cigarettes. We had all the cigarettes in the jail. The core group was me, Lobo, Juan Valez, T.C., and Jim, along with the three river rats, but we let some of the locals join us, the really big guys. We always recruited the big guys. "Hey, George! You can be friends with us! C'mon upstairs and play cards with us!"

One day I finally got even with Lobo for the cigarette he flipped into my shirt on the way to Berkeley back in January. We were playing cards and I was smoking. Lobo was wearing a wool shirt. When he looked away for a second I reached over and put the lit cigarette in his pocket. A few minutes later he jumped up howling and patting his chest. I broke out laughing and Lobo reached over to this small table where the peanut butter and jelly was kept in jars. He grabbed a big glob of jelly and threw it at me. I grabbed the peanut butter and threw it at him. There followed a huge food fight where we smeared the whole place.

Visiting time was a kick. The visiting room was about the size of a bedroom, but the guards didn't look in that often. Plus, you could sit in a corner where they couldn't see you at all. So, we got in the corner when the girls came to visit and bring us our cigarettes. After they left, we had a couple more cartons of cigarettes to win more cigarettes with. Whoever else got presents on visiting day came up to the library and immediately lost them to us.

The girls also brought us vials of whiskey, so we'd get bullshit in the corner. By the time we returned to our cells, we were drunk on our butts. Meanwhile, T.C. was on the floor fucking his ol' lady, who didn't wear any panties for the occasion. We stood around so no one could see.

One day two FBI agents came to speak with Lobo and me because we were supposedly running guns to the Quebec Liberation Front. They claimed they had pictures of me driving murder vehicles, and all kinds of bullshit. They showed me 12 million snapshots taken by none other than *the bus Fed from the Park!* This was the guy the Hog Farmers defended and allowed to live in the Park. Now, here were the pictures he'd taken of all the people in the Park just about a month before. So, the FBI showed me pictures of all my friends at the Park and said, "You know this person, what's his name?"

"I don't know that person."

"Do you know *this* person?"

"I don't know him. Give me a coffee, man."

"Do you know *this* person? Do you know *this* person? Do you know *this* person?"

They showed me a picture of myself. "Do you know *this* person?"

"No idea."

They showed me a picture of Lobo. "Do you know *this* person?"

"Never saw that person in my life."

"You don't seem to know *anybody*, do you?"

"Naw, man, I don't even know who the fuck I am. I just had a head injury and I can't seem to remember anything."

"Do you know anything about a supermarket that was robbed about two months ago?"

"I don't know anything about it."

"Do you know anything about 40 cases of rifles that were taken? You know anything about the Quebec Liberation Front?"

"I know Quebec's somewhere's up north, that's all I know."

"Have you ever seen this van before?"

"No."

"Weren't you in this van just before you were arrested?"

"No, I wasn't."

"We have *pictures* of you driving this van."

"No, you don't."

"This van was involved in a murder in New York State. You're going to be an accessory to murder if you don't tell us the truth."

"I don't know anything about it."

"Do you know Michael Dodge?"

"Who?"

"Michael Dodge."

"Never heard of him."

"You've been seen with him around Island Pond and St. Johnsbury all the time."

"I don't know what the fuck you're talking about, man. Listen, could you get me a cup of coffee? Just knock on the door and ask the guard for a cup of coffee."

They got me a cup of coffee and I drank it down. "Will you get me another cup of coffee, man?"

Eventually I convinced them I was in the hospital and was in no condition to be driving any murder vehicles around. I never heard of the Quebec Liberation Front. I never heard the word "Revolution." I didn't know a damn thing. They gave up on me.

Then they called in Lobo and asked him the same questions. He just refused to talk to them.

Well, that visit upped us to the top of the jail hierarchy. You had to be bad dudes to get a visit from the FBI, so we benefited from their visit. Plus, our suspicions were confirmed about the narc the Hog Farmers protected, those stupid fucks!

Eventually, our 20 days were up and most of us were released, although Lobo had about 12 more to go. That night Juan, T.C., and me were wandering around St. Johnsbury and we went into a local bar. One of the guards was there and he came over to me and said, "*Please, never get arrested in this town again!*"

"You guys are the ones making the arrests," I said, "not me."

Later, T.C. and me were walking down the street and we saw some local yokels fighting with the three river rats. One of the locals pointed at T.C. and said, "Look, there's that damn nigger who fucks the white whore! We're the Smith Brothers! We're the baddest motherfuckers in Vermont! We own this town! Get the fuck off the sidewalk!" One of these Smith Brothers pulled out his little knife, waved it at T.C. and said, "I'm gonna cut your big fat nose off, nigger!"

T.C. had a little pouch behind his neck in which he carried a big knife. He whipped it out and, quick as Zorro, sliced that fucker's face open from cheek to cheek. Blood spurted everywhere. The fucker started screaming, "I'm bleeding! I'm bleeding!"

Suddenly the cops appeared. Another brouhaha, but since there were witnesses that the Smith Brother pulled a knife first, they let us go. They just told us to get the fuck out of St. Johnsbury.

So, we went on back to the Park to wait for Lobo to get out of jail. Bernie was staying in the A-frame, so we moved in with him. In the meantime, Cocaine and Sally Saucerhead had come up from Cambridge. We'd been running into these two girls everywhere, from Berkeley to Harvard Square for quite a while. Since Abbe wasn't around, I hooked up with Sally, so I at least had somebody to fuck. Sally sat on my face for 45-minutes while everybody milled around, watching, and Juan Valez wailed away on some bongos while yelling, "Yeah, man, eat that pussy!" After about a week of muff diving and getting drunk, the girls went back down to Cambridge.

One day Bernie, Juan, T.C., and me got especially drunk. We hopped the train that went by the Park and ended up in Island Puddle. We ran into a friend who had a gallon of wine. We chugged that and went into a store to get another. I was in the back of the store checking out the situation preparatory to lifting a couple of bottles of wine when I saw the clerk grab a crowbar and try to smash T.C. in the head. T.C. had been caught yet again trying to boost something. They started fighting and another guy jumped on T.C., so I jumped on him. All kinds of hell broke loose as we trashed that store. The clerk dropped the crowbar. I grabbed it up as the clerk ran for the phone on the wall. I ran after him and smashed the phone off the wall.

The local sheriff in Island Puddle was Danny Cross. He hated everyone at the Park. He suddenly appeared with a State Trooper. They came *in* the door just as the fight rolled *out* the door. There was a big scuffle and Cross yelled, "Morgan!

Get your fucking ass out of here!" I smashed him right in the face. He fell to the ground and I started kicking the shit out of him. Meanwhile, Bernie had the State Trooper. Juan was just standing around screaming, "Viva la Revolution!"

The State Trooper was yelling, "You're under arrest! You're under arrest!" So, I ran over and hit the motherfucker. I figured I was under arrest anyway for kicking in the sheriff's ribs, who was still lying on the sidewalk groaning. Bernie started kicking the Trooper in the kidneys. Somehow he got his hand down to his belt and sprayed us all with Mace. I got it full in the face, so we backed off to clear our eyes. T.C. was rolling on the ground, gagging from the stuff.

In the distance I saw an army of State Troopers coming. I put my head down and ran full into that Statie, hitting him in the stomach and knocking him on his ass, and I took off. The train station was right across the street and the train that had brought us in was starting out, so Juan, Bernie, and me made for it. I thought T.C. was right behind us, but he was still rolling on the ground in front of the store, gagging and rubbing his eyes. I was just waiting for the Statie to shoot me in the back. I mean, how long does it take for the fucker to get his gun out, y'know? Instead, the fucker was dumb enough to chase us!

We jumped on the train and the Statie was right behind us. He reached up to grab Bernie's leg. Bernie kicked him in the face. The dude was running right next to the train and down he went, rolling in the gravel. Meanwhile, all the other Staties had gotten out of their cars with their shotguns and were yelling for the train to stop.

The train started to slow down, so we climbed onto the other side, jumped off, and ran into the woods and up a hill. Bernie and Juan took off, but I couldn't breathe because of the fucking Mace. My eyes were full of tears and my throat hurt like hell, so, I crawled into a pile of leaves, dug a hole, and covered myself with the leaves. I heard the Staties running all over the place looking for us. After things quieted down, I crawled out and climbed to the top of the hill.

I found Bernie and Juan and we started walking along these back roads. Some cop cars roared up the road and we jumped off the road into the woods. Bernie went to the right and quickly got caught. Juan and me went to the left and jumped over a small hedge. There was a ten-foot drop on the other side into a driveway leading into a garage. I ran into the garage looking for a place to hide. In the corner was a Briggs and Stratton 3-hp lawnmower, the kind you rode, which I hunkered down behind. I pulled some junk over me to conceal myself. Then Juan ran in and crawled under some junk.

Then here came a posse of Vermont farmers with their shotguns. I guess the whole town of Island Pond was after us. "Where'd them God-damned hippies go?" They came into the garage with flashlights and looked all over the place.

"We caught one, but there's two more of them bastards around someplace." I was waiting to be tarred and feathered or lynched or something -- and I didn't know what for!

The posse eventually ambled off. I didn't know if they'd quit looking for us, so I laid there for about nine hours. I didn't move a muscle till it started getting dark. Juan didn't move a muscle, either, though I heard him swearing in Puerto Rican over in the corner. He kept whispering, "Pssst! Let's get outta here!"

I whispered back, "No! They might still be out there!"

We finally crawled out about nine o'clock at night. We began creeping down the road, ready to jump in the bushes at any moment. Every time a car came, we dived off the road. We were going to walk the railroad tracks all the way back up to the Park, about 35 miles. We walked the tracks for quite a ways. Then we got out on a road. A car came by and we jumped in the bushes. As it drove by, I noticed it was friends of mine, Brad and Diane, the couple that had rescued me from the hospital, so I ran out in the road yelling, "Stop! Stop!" Luckily, they heard me and stopped.

We hopped in and told them the story. They told us what was happening back in Island Pond. They said there was a mob of farmers with shotguns in front of the store waiting for dogs to track us with.

At the Park we went up to the A-frame, which is in the back of the Park. There was a little trail called "Rabbit Alley" leading to it. Once past the A-frame the trail continued on toward the Canadian border. That day, every time someone came to the Park, someone ran back and yelled, "Cops! Cops!"

Juan and me jumped out of the A-frame and booked up Rabbit Alley as far as we could, slogging through the mud, and hid. All the time we thought we heard people yelling, "There they go! Blast'em!" Then someone would come back and say, "Oh, it was nobody." We did that about ten times, then said to hell with it.

Somehow, Bernie got out of it all and showed up at the Park. They kept T.C., and I never saw him again. We hung out in the Park for a while, getting drunk, still waiting for Lobo to be released. A few days later Lobo showed up and we decided to head back down to Cambridge, as it had become too hot for us in that area.

So, we spilt into small parties. Bernie, Lobo, and me were one party; the other was Juan and Blackberry. I was very paranoid about hitchhiking through Island Pond, but we had to do it because it was the only way out of there. We got a ride *right into* Island Pond, but I talked the guy into letting us out on the far side of town. Then a car picked us up and took us straight to Harvard Square. Juan and Blackberry showed up later that night.

And that was how, in the fall of 1973, we left Earth People's Park.

Afterword

Morgan and Abbe now live in California in wedded bliss.

If you enjoyed this memoir, read more about
Morgan's life on the streets in:

Road Rabble
A Street Memoir of the Seventies
By
Morgan M. Morgan

and

Orphans of the Storm
A Shared Memoir of the Radical Seventies
By
Morgan M. Morgan, et al.